MORE SILLY SIGNS

MORE
SILLY SIGNS

THE MAD, THE BAD AND THE WEIRD

TIM GLYNNE-JONES

AURA

AURA

This edition published in 2019
by Baker & Taylor (UK) Ltd,
Bicester, Oxfordshire, OX26 4ST

ISBN: 978-1-78888-933-9
AD006630UK

Printed in China

Signs are vital. Signs are essential. Signs are hilarious when they don't quite get the message right. All around the world, silly signs are spotted every day and they come in many forms. There are the signs where the grasp of English has just fallen short with comical consequences, signs where the meaning is understood but the double meaning is much more amusing, signs where the writer has set out to be funny and succeeded, and signs where a picture paints a thousand words, none of which seem to make any sense.

In this book you'll find examples of all the above, from the invitation to 'drop your trousers here' to the barber's shop that proudly goes by the name of 'Wiggy's'. There are street names, road signs, animal signs, warning signs, shop signs, toilet signs, restaurant signs ... and in every case there are signs that all is not quite right. We have to thank the good folk who take the trouble to put up signs. They help us on our way safely and happily through life and they keep us laughing throughout the journey.

Have you seen
this dog?

I have now

Yeah! In my nightmares . . .

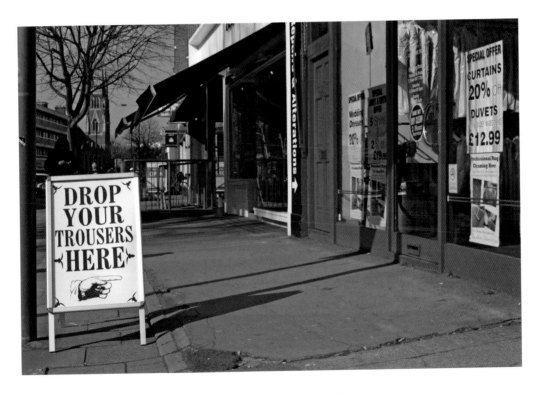

Business suddenly seemed to dry up

Risk of sudden wind

The Clean Air Act is taken very seriously here

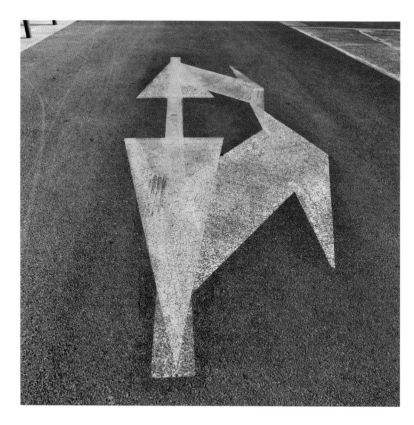

Just don't turn left, OK?

Funny, I'm sure it said that yesterday

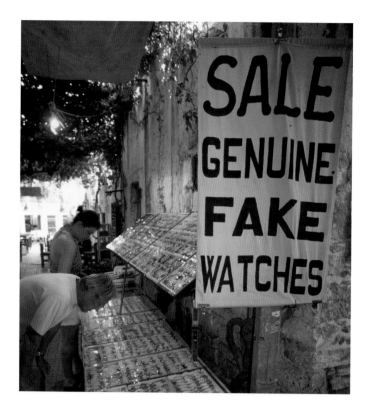

None of your cheap imitations, these are the real deal

I predict you're for the chop

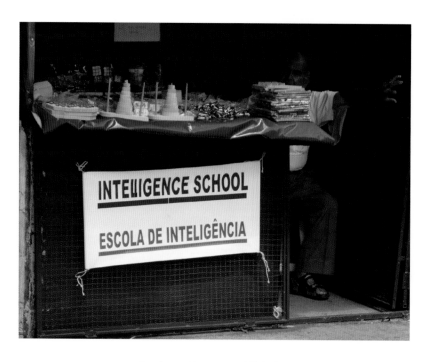

So clever they named it twice

THIS SIGN IS IN SPANISH WHEN YOU'RE NOT LOOKING

Or is it?

Answers to the name of Badger

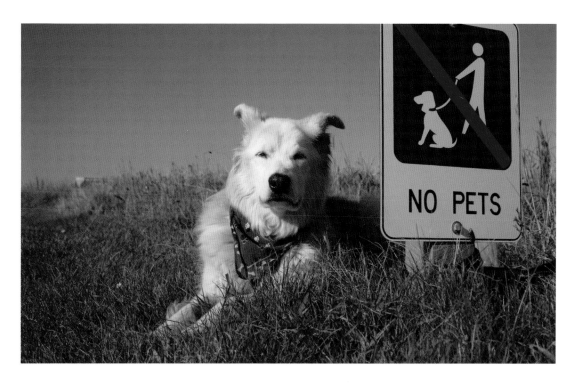

'I vont to be alone'

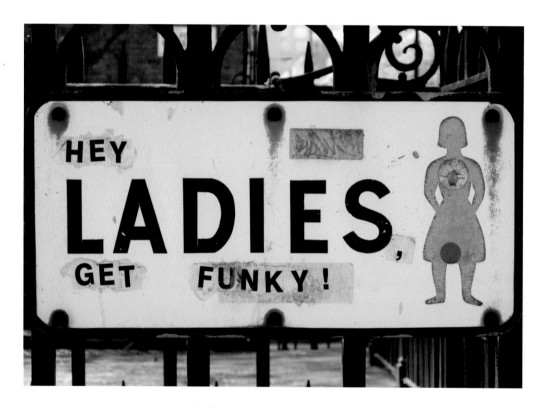

Like they say – don't get mad . . .

And finish using restroom before returning to car!

Make sure you have someone watching

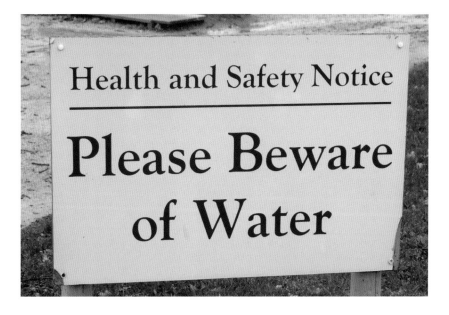

Health and Safety Notice

Please Beware of Water

Well, you can't say they don't warn you

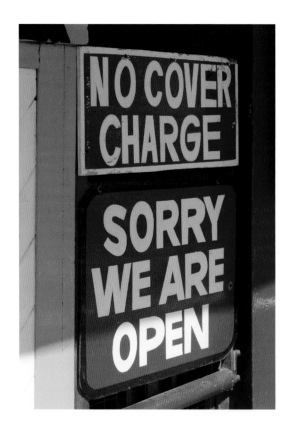

HQ of the Society for People With Low Self-Esteem

You hum it, I'll thing it

So that's why they call it the funny farm

トイレを綺麗にご使用下さい。

Please use a toilet finely.

请 清 洁 的 使 用 厕 所

화장실을 예쁘게 사용해 주십시오

鹿 苑 寺

It's perfectionism gone mad!

Camels only welcome on Wednesdays

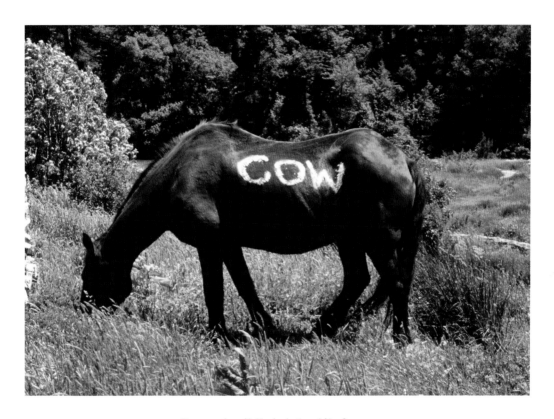

Rumour has it that she's a bit of a nag

The touchy-feely approach to security

It's one of life's incontrovertible truths

雷雨天气 禁打手机

SPEAKING CELLPHONE IS STRICTLY PROHIBITED WHEN THUNDERSTORM

Is it a crossword clue?

Spread your own

If it's always nice, then I'll always take it

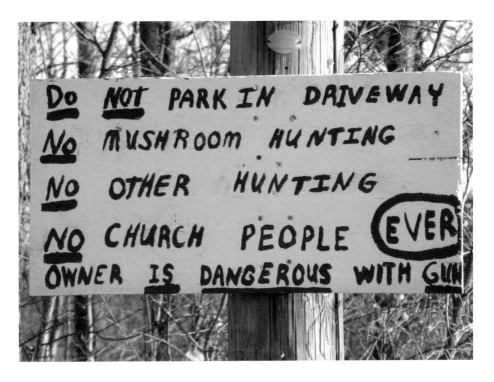

This outfit needs to rethink its advertising

And if your dog poos on the ice?

. . . and their filthy habits

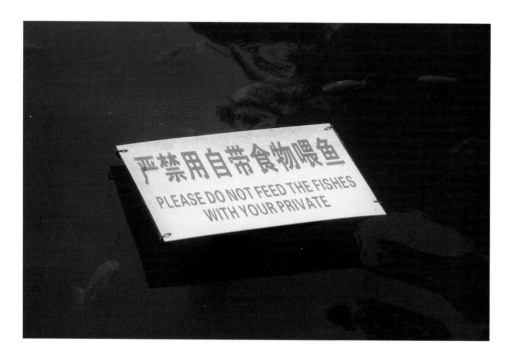

严禁用自带食物喂鱼

PLEASE DO NOT FEED THE FISHES WITH YOUR PRIVATE

Who ordered the prawn balls?

PUBLIC
DRINKING WATER
OUTSIDE
LADIES & GENTS
TOILETS

Hmm, think I'll pass

Today's Summer Fun has been cancelled

We will try to rearrange

But don't hold your breath

I'm only going to say this once

This is not the free world

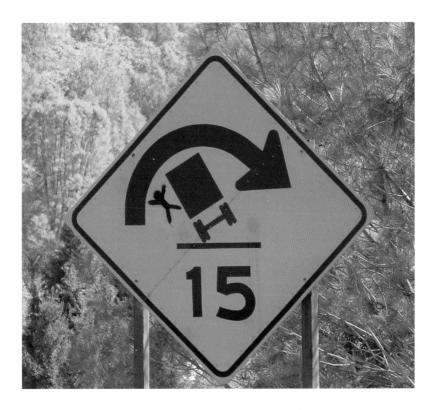

Please fall out of your lorry on the right?

It's one of the quieter beaches in the county

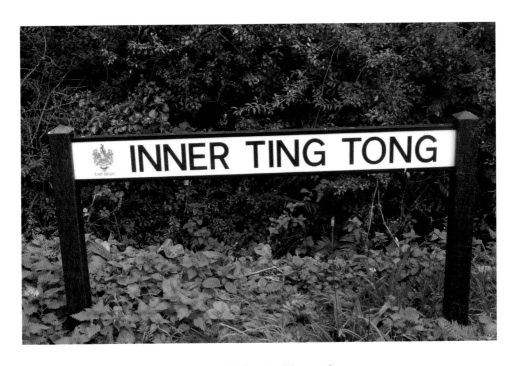

Are you in touch with yours?

Feeling lucky, punk?

Well, are ya...?

The local watchmaker wondered why business was slow

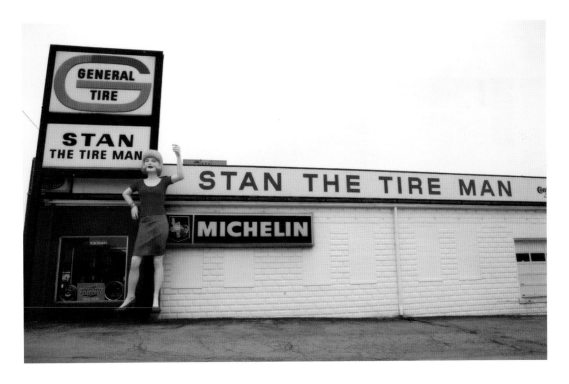

You might notice a change in Stan

Permissive Footpath

It's neither straight nor narrow

Sharing is caring

Home of the mad cow

While-u-wait?

请勿倚靠

DO NOT RELY ON

Anyone? Anything? . . . We need to know!

Beware - existentialist poet ahead

The choice, dear reader, is yours

Empty it in the children's play area like everyone else

Not if I dig you first

We're a cold-hearted bunch

男 厠
MENS
RETS ROOM

Reserved for the bets of the rets?

It was a kind of calling

My dog can attack in fluent French

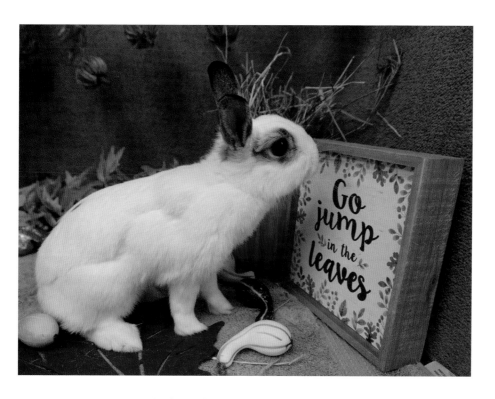

You know, that's really not a bad idea!

Just not in the mood for company right now

The rates are astronomical!

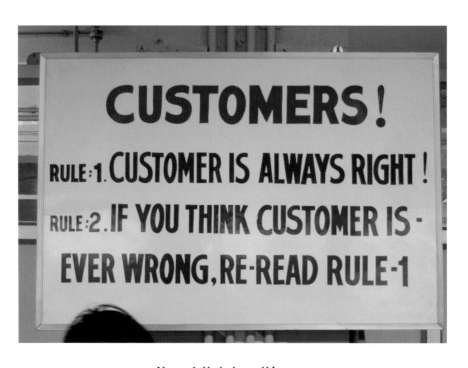

Ah good, that clears things up

Why they invented punctuation

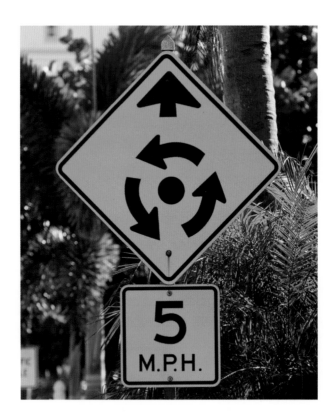

Going slowly round the bend?

But do not approach under any circumstances

No mention of what to do if confronted by one

Ah! Maybe that's the answer!

The fashionable end of town

And the less fashionable end

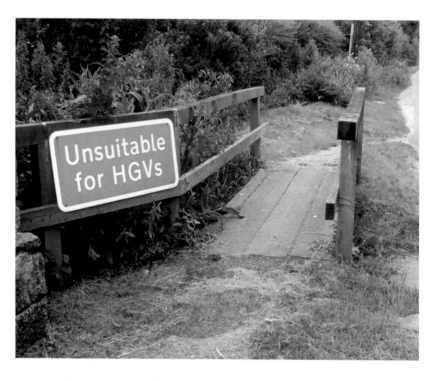

Please use alternative route . . . a couple of feet to the right

The omnibus edition of this sign will be shown on Sunday

免费卫生纸
请珍惜使用

**FREE TOILET PAPER
PLEASE CHERISH
THE USE**

Yeah – show some gratitude!

The number of bodies is up to you

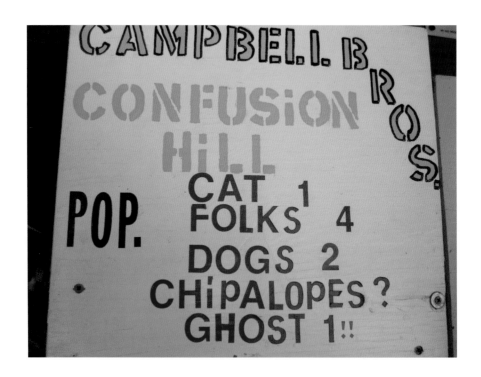

Everyone else left town years ago

Fancy a spa treatment with your wifi?

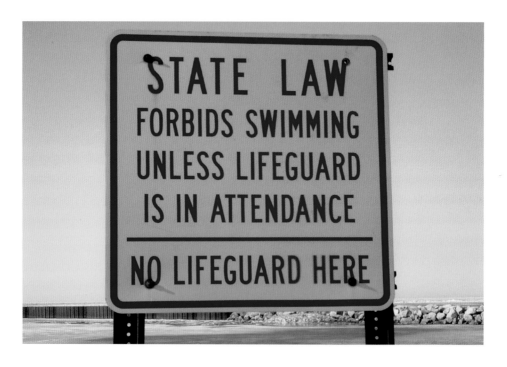

STATE LAW
FORBIDS SWIMMING
UNLESS LIFEGUARD
IS IN ATTENDANCE

NO LIFEGUARD HERE

Therefore . . .

Words fail me. And the writer of this sign!

Under abduction?

Well, nobody's perfect

Understanding the mindset of the modern dog owner

Must have lost the remote

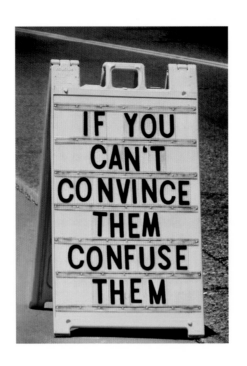

The first rule of advertising

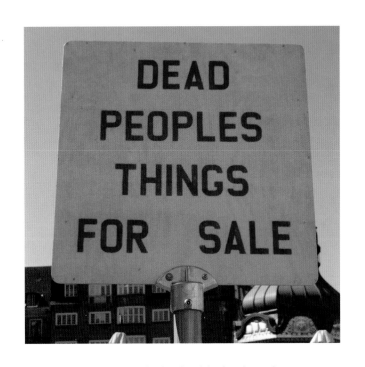

The second rule: don't be too honest

How many do you have?

Narcissists say it's the only place to shop

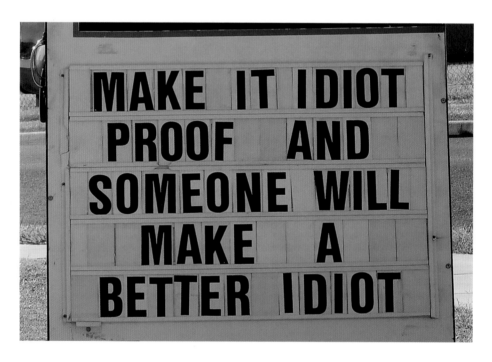

One of life's little ironies

Yes – that Jacky

Try the giraffe house

Be quick, or hop it!

The third rule of advertising: manage expectations . . .

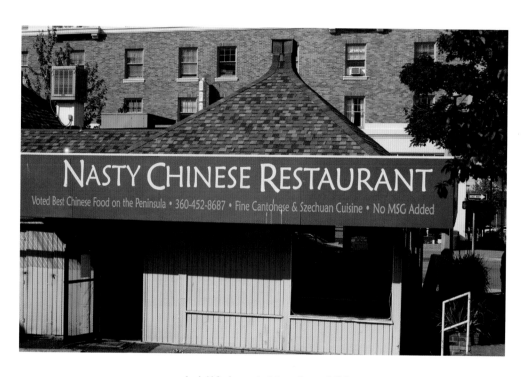

NASTY CHINESE RESTAURANT
Voted Best Chinese Food on the Peninsula • 360-452-8687 • Fine Cantonese & Szechuan Cuisine • No MSG Added

. . . but this is probably going a bit far

That's going to be a tricky tee shot!

THERE ARE NO HORSES LEFT ON THIS VAN AT NIGHT

We've left them with the neigh-bours

What more do you need?

This is cobblers

Maybe I'll pass on that pole-dancing class

Heavy lifting makes you fart?

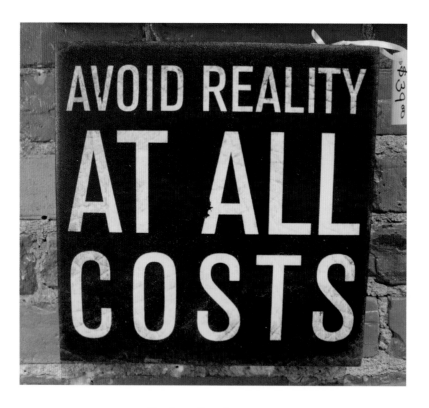

You know it makes sense

Ever felt your life was going in the wrong direction?

No overacting

The outlet for well-mannered lads – a niche market

Maybe ease up on the wine?

You do the math

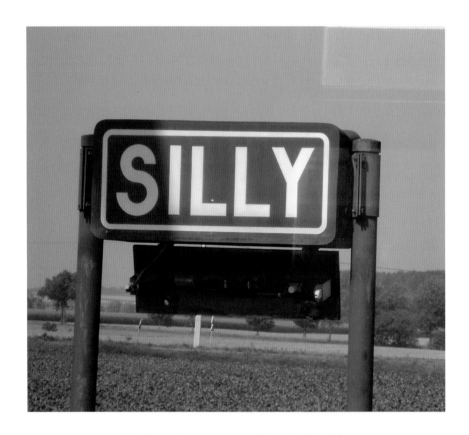

You know where you are with a sign like this

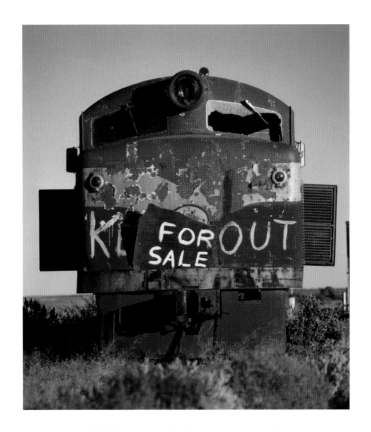

Did they run out of track - or steam?

In case of emergency - seek a cryptologist

The term 'green consumer' takes on a new meaning

Remind me, does a red circle mean it's forbidden or compulsory?

All dogs allowed - except Goofy

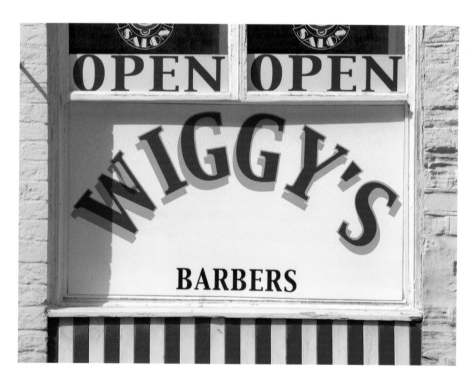

We know all the short cuts

For the defeatist DIYer

Please put your littl'uns in the bin provided

Step On The Pedal?

We try . . . but after four glasses of pastis we just speak rubbish

You'll find 'smarty' panties in aisle two

They're queueing around the block for this

小草含羞笑
请君莫打扰

Tiny grass is shyly smiling and would not like to be interrupted.

Keep off the grass (unlike the signwriter)

Choose life

Dolphin riding is not for the uninitiated

Flight or fight?

Consonant please, Rachel . . .

They pee on the seats

My pet's been lying to me since 1996

Looks like a trap

Everything must go. Including me!

Picture Credits